I Spy
Fairytales

Written by Charlotte Raby
and Emily Guille-Marrett
Illustrated by Deborah Partington

Collins

4

6

8

 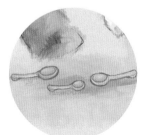 

10

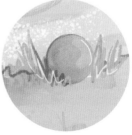

12

Match the lost items

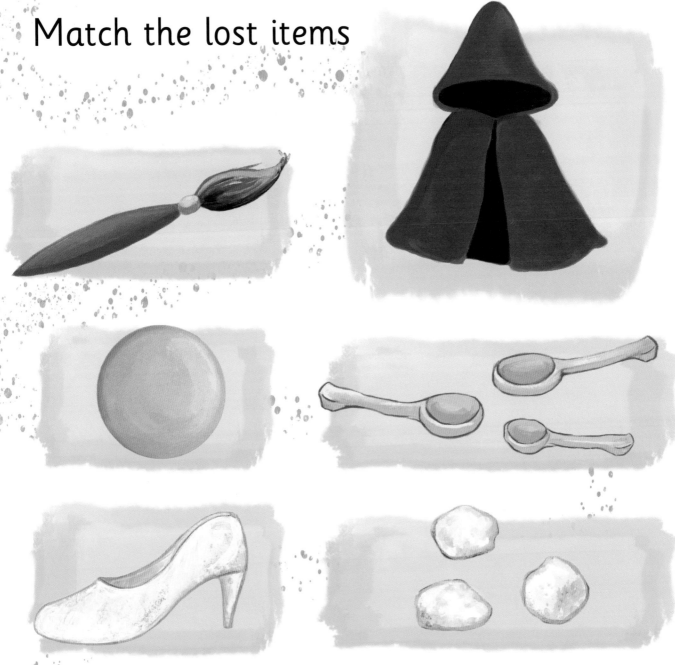

🐾 Review: After reading 🐾

Read 1: Decoding
- Look at one of the scenes together. Play 'I spy' with the children, putting a lot of emphasis on the initial sound, e.g. on page 3, 'I spy with my little eye, something beginning with "a".' (*axe*). Play this game with the other scenes too, taking turns to spy things in the pictures.

Read 2: Prosody
- Encourage the children to hold the book and to turn the pages.
- Look at the pictures together and ask them to tell each of the fairy tales in their own words.

Read 3: Comprehension
- Ask the children to find the item that each character drops and make sure they notice that the girl picks that item up in the next scene.
- Explore the final scene together and discuss which items have now been returned to their owners. Make sure the children understand that the girl returns to her own world at the end of the book.
- Turn to pages 14 and 15 and ask the children to match up the character with the item that belongs to them, returning back to the story for support where needed.
- Ask the children:
  o Which one of the fairy tales in the book do you like the most? Why?
  o What is your favourite part of that fairy tale?
  o Can you think of another ending for that fairy tale?